South of Serenity

A Poet's Quest

South of Serenity

A Poet's Quest

Ray Hamilton

Living the Poem
Rehoboth Beach, Delaware

CONTENTS

ACKNOWLEDGEMENTS

I want to take the time to acknowledge the Spirit of the Universe for creating this book and placing these people in my life to help bring it to fruition. Without them, it would not have been possible.

Aunt Belinda (my mother's sister): She has always had a place in her heart for my spirit. She was the only lifeline I had at the lowest, darkest time in my life. I have to laugh when I think of this fine Christian woman going out of her way to type up the tainted poetry from her black sheep nephew and smuggle it back into prison to me. Her efforts were the foundation of this book. Her husband, Edward, was a guardian angel and positive role model who always made me feel comfortable.

Uncle Dale (my mother's brother): By far, he is the most humble, positive role model of a man I've ever met. He and his wife, Christine, took me in and tried to give me a better life. Guardian angels.

Zach (my son): I'm so proud of the man he has become. Nothing makes a father happier than to know his son has become good people. Thanks for your help in editing the book. Your insights led to major changes in the end result. I love and believe in you.

Mom: I don't worry about you reading the final copy, I know you helped me write it. Love and miss you and will carry your spirit with me every day.

Kim Sturgis: Thank you for the countless hours of typing and editing and re-editing with me hovering over your shoulder pushing perfection.

Steve Robison: The key ingredient. The last piece of the puzzle. The final editor, my publisher, friend, and fellow poet who believed in me and my work and was willing to take it to the next level. I was awaiting his arrival for years. Thank you for your service to the universe. I couldn't have done it without you.

I drew the artwork on the cover when I was in prison. I had written, maybe, three poems. But I knew then it was going to be on the cover of my fancied book. The picture is a self-portrait of what goes on in my head.

1 THE BURDEN OF POTENTIAL

NOTE TO SELF

Today and tomorrow, one and the same.

Don't get distracted with fortune and fame.

Respecting the bottom. Reaching for the top.

Creates momentum that no one can stop.

Expressions from the heart. Fuel for the mind.

Follow your talent. Leave a legacy behind.

FORECASTING

Frosty morning, lion's den.
Warped mind, lonely pen.
Morning dew, ending night.
Addict or not, continue to write.

Several Xanax, couple of joints.
Finally reached a turning point.
One day's hope: can learn to deal.
All these emotions I refuse to feel.

Addicted to everything under the sun.
Hell with reality, rather run.
Fear of success raging inside.
Run on self-will. No place to hide

Confronted by truth. Bitter and mean.
New obsession, write myself clean.
Something attractive. Find a wife.
Into the sunset, poetic life.

BURDEN OF POTENTIAL

Contemplating depths that aren't really there.
While basking the emptiness of a blank stare.
Free the mind from this vegetative state.
Makes discipline such an important date.

Following a skill will always provide proof.
There's honor and courage in seeking truth.
Sedated for years. I've done all but feel.
Pain of this world that's become too real.

A burden of potential placed upon my heart.
Disease of addiction manifesting through art.
Fingers are discolored, stained with nicotine.
Strung out on writing. I'm still just a fiend.

Living life on life's terms, at times gets rough.
One's too many. A thousand not enough.
Unwilling to drown–reaching for the top
Obsession and compulsion. Just can't stop.

CREATION

I have no excuse.
The muse has gone away.
It's only through discipline,
I can write today.

Day without fire,
Opportunity to slave.
Willing to chase talent
up and beyond my grave.

In active addiction,
it's the poet's fix.
When the pencil and paper
begin performing tricks.

Ending with something
where nothing's involved.
Creation is no more
than a problem solved.

MENTAL MASTURBATION

Poetic license.
Way to discover means.
Create a dimension.
Linking reality with dreams.
Chasing fragments.
That dance in my head.
Night succeeding night,
as I lie here in bed.
At times nothing more
Than mental masturbation.
Best and worst of
subconscious conversations.
Poems are like comets
streaking the sky.
they begin to flash.
I hook them going by.
A creative process
of which I'm so fond.
Pulling a prize fish
from a polluted pond.

WRITER'S BLOCK

Couldn't resist the Master's call.

Plans that were made, dropped them all.

For miles I walked along the beach.

Chasing a fragment just out of reach.

Saw a jetty through the ocean's glare.

Following the mist until I was there.

Elusive fragment. Thought it through.

Under a vast sky so deeply blue.

Surprised how things were coming together.

The mood I was in, never been better.

It was going to be a special night.

Pulitzer Prize winning poem I'd write.

Everything was perfect. Could no longer wait.

What I would write was going to be great.

Then realized I was the butt of a joke.

Pulled out my pencil…the point was broke!

Wanted to frown but wasn't sad

Kind of funny. I'd been had.

Looking up knowing I wasn't alone.

Smile on my face, I headed home.

I AM

Twisting and turning,
In me the seagulls play.
Cool ocean breeze.
Ending hot summer day.

Explorer of nature.
Untamed, roaming free.
Golden sunset.
Dipped into the sea.

Descending star
with amber glow.
all the colors
of a falling rainbow.

Reaching for the heavens
where my salvation sits.
I am the poet.
Finally, a hat that fits.

DEBUT

First, they were restless.
Extremely loud.
Thought to myself,
"What an unruly crowd."
Place full of temperament,
ego and pride.
Front and center.
Revealed a softer side.
Expecting to be
run off the floor.
When finished,
they wanted more.
Moment became surreal
in County Jail.
Inmates attentive
like students at Yale.
Monumental day.
Conquered those fears.
Reciting my work
in front of peers.

Poem read well…
with rhythm and flow.
From attentive crowd,
received a Standing O!

STARVING ARTIST

Out of light, into dark.
Brilliant writer left her mark.
Seeking acceptance from her peers,
Lead to lonely nights full of fears.

She reached a point of total disgust.
Having no one to love, no one to trust.
People of the time labeled her strange.
Talent alone has developed its range.

Life has ended, only the work will remain.
Searching for beauty she discovered pain.
Through death a star was born.
Leaving the art… a world in mourn.

Life is over before it would begin.
Gave it her all…tried fitting in.
Lack of acceptance changed her direction.
Final blow to a fear of rejection.

Our community put to the test.

Starving artist been laid to rest.

Somehow, lost the desire to create,

Last meal was the bullet she ate.

DYING IN VAIN

Most have their rhythm.
Followed with flow.
Some of them wilt.
While others grow.

They are about beauty.
Touch of creation.
Falling to the ground.
Chasing salvation.

Finding your depth.
Exploring new heights.
Busting your ass
Working long nights.

Hope one day.
The whole world will see.
My love for the poem
The manic in me.

Lifetime obsession
My sheltered pain.
Will I meet success?
Or die in vain?

2 FANCY JACKETS

MOTHER

Above the surface seems nothing's wrong
Down below the currents strong
Unable to comprehend love and affection
Mom's been pulled in every direction

Innocence stolen at such a young age
Grandmom's blindness becomes her rage
Too painful to bear, hides from the past
Tried to end it all with a shotgun blast

Escape with Lady Heroin has its price
Everything she loved becomes sacrificed
No one understands. Magnitude of shame
Wrote her off. Labeled insane

Hopelessness in her eyes, tight clenching fists
Tried to hide, I saw her gaping wrists.
Another failed attempt at suicide
Brand new scars she'll have to hide

Life at times cold as steel.
Now older your pain I feel
Have another chance to live again
Can we conquer these demons within?

Been hopeful. Dreams have come true
Blessing me—you continue to pull through
Please don't checkout. Need you to remain.
Life without you—could not bear such pain.

FINALLY FREE

I was a boy. Barely knew my dad.
Sentenced to life. Robbery gone bad.
Police showed up. Snatched him from me.
Convicted of murder in the first degree.

Devastated, miserably sad.
So many years. Missed my dad.
Loved this man. His absence deeply felt.
Tears rolling down at the hand I was dealt.

Would smile as if everything's okay.
Down inside, heart ripped away.
Praying hard through the fear.
Hoping one day my step he'd appear.

Doing things. Defying common sense.
Reality set in—he'd stay behind the fence.
Served many years of straight time.
Insanity crept in. He lost his mind.

He could not stand one more day.
Cried out, "God, is there a different way?"
Nodded his head as if to say okay.
Lights out, slowly passed away.

Never turns out how I want it to be.
Ashes in an urn returned to me.
Took and released them into the sea.
After all these years dad was finally free.

TORN

Passionate mother ravaged with emotional scars.
Dad's last years on earth, spent behind bars.
Thinking of the innocent blood Father spilled.
I pray for the family of the man he killed.

Received a letter, haunting piece of mail.
Said my best friend had been raped in jail.
Another family member diagnosed with HIV.
Brother Mike overdosed… leaving without me.

Favorite cousin, Wade, shot with a forty-four.
Died in father's arms, yards from mom's door.
After many years of marriage, uncle's a survivor
Wife had been killed, victim of a drunk driver.

My aunt's first baby died the day I was born.
Trying to be whole. Damn, I've been torn.
Convicted felon. Half my life on the run.
Forgive me Master… I have come undone.

STRIFE

Afraid of day. Consumed by night.
Dropped out of school. Learned how to fight.
Hanging out late. Following wrong crowds.
Rejecting authority. Head in the clouds.

Needing a chemical just to get through.
Doing things never imagined I'd do.
Running in the rain. Stomping through puddles.
Choices I've made came with these struggles.

Sex, drugs, rock -n- roll.
Didn't take long, lost control.
Couldn't keep track of my own sins.
Detached, from family and friends.

Watched streets swallow a person's soul.
Witnessed a disease take its toll.
Life has been hard. No fairy tale.
Mom has a disease. Dad died in jail.

Been everywhere without leaving the hood.

Not that I'm dangerous, just misunderstood.

Nothing's been more consistent in life.

Then the recurrence of pain and strife.

FRIENDSHIP

Friends, I look forward to seeing.
Pray for their health and well-being.
Friends can be helpful, lifting a frown.
Pick you up when you're feeling down

Not easy being a true friend
Must work hard beginning to end
Unconditional love—a giant task
Most will run once I remove my mask

Painful watching me self-destruct.
Wonder why my friendships erupt?
Not many have endured—few remain.
Friendships dwindle like a flickering flame.

THE RACIST

Not writing just to cover a page.
Taught to hate; such a young age.
Look through my eyes; perception of you.
What I'm thinking—probably not true.

Have to admit, hatred endured the season.
Stereotyping people without a reason.
Many different races beneath our sun.
What will it take for us to become one?

Controlled by my fears, perceptions wrong.
What am I waiting for? Why's it taking so long?
How long before I swallow my pride?
A better place when we put differences aside.

Broaden horizons. Brighten skies.
New perception seen through your eyes.
To be authentic. Can no longer fake.
Heart of the matter. Old habits hard to break.

Faith, forgiveness, grace to be strong.

Shortcoming of mine's held so long.

Know only the truth shall set me free.

"Please remove the racist in me."

DROPLETS OF RAIN

No one knows what we're fighting for.
Most of the world… stationed at war.
On September 11, towers fell from the sky.
Plane hit the Pentagon. We wondered why.

Peace is not here nor there.
Toxic substances polluting our air.
Inner cities and towns under attack.
Not just from terrorism. Also, from crack.

Global warming starts sounding alarms.
Country sides littered with withering farms.
Famine and disease devastate foreign lands.
Erosion intensifies – stripping beaches of sand.

Natural disasters show their face.
Thousands dead, millions displaced.
Wildfires burn forests to the ground.
Search for answers. None to be found.

Signs of the time make my eyes leak.

Tsunamis alone killed thousands this week.

Try to be strong, feel the world's pain.

My tear drops fall like droplets of rain.

ALL PARTIES INVOLVED

Leaving behind families
they love and adore.
Praying for their soldiers
headed off to war.

Courage and bravery
beginning to shine.
Comfort the souls
they're leaving behind.

Thousands shipped out
to a foreign land.
Hope a safe return
part of the plan.

Terrorism lingering.
War in the air.
Entire human race
desperate need of prayer.

Don't think our differences
will be peacefully solved
All I can do is pray
for all parties involved.

DEPRESSED

Future's close. Seems far away.
Burdens I bear… heavy today.
Woke up with pain inside my head.
Buzzards circling. They think I'm dead.

Bi-polar. Spiraling down.
Single expression. Stuck on a frown.
Radio plays. Hate my favorite song.
Today is just taking too long.

Emotions run wild. I've lost control.
Helplessness, takes its toll.
Goals and dreams, out of sight.
Search darkness for a shimmer of light.

Mental illness destroyed my family tree.
Pray to God it stops with me.
Look for energy already spent.
Today's death a welcomed event.

Darkness shadowed perception of things.
Paralyzed by depression. Pain it brings.
Been gray. Struggle to get through.
Maybe tomorrow sky will be blue.

AUTUMN'S GLORY

Can't explain or find a reason.
So affected by this changing season.
In autumn's glory I go insane
trying to medicate a phantom pain.

Know it's the end to a cycle of life.
Begin creating havoc, chaos and strife.
Surrounded by beauty, emotions erupt.
After the colors peak, I self-destruct.

Couple of beers, few tokes from the bong.
Before I know it, in search of something strong.
The journey has begun; sold my soul.
Slipping down this dark dinghy hole.

Undetected, beneath the radar.
Stranger appears, jumps in the car.
Reaches down deep in his socks
Reveals to me a large bag of rocks.

Heart begins to race, body starts shaking
in anticipation of the hit I'll be taking.
Find a secluded spot, take my first blast.
Wow! What a rush, fading so fast.

Now in my system this chemical I crave.
Within a few minutes, have become a slave
Day turns to night and day again
Stranger has become my only friend.

Spend everything I own, now I'm broke.
Dealer vanished, friendship a joke.
Hopelessness, guilt and bitter remorse
It happened so fast…drifted off course.

Search for means, a way to get more
Fiending; out of crack, I enter a store
Cross the line into pure white trash
Over the counter, I snatch the cash.

Everything I love sacrificed so fast.

Hoping the next hit would be my last.

Pain of disgrace all I could feel.

What was phantom has become real.

Life has meaning, my story I'll tell.

Dancing with the devil, landed in hell.

Stuck in this cage, Rehabilitating my fury.

Hidden from Autumn in all its glory.

Through it all, obtained something to give

Instead of wilting, a desire to live.

FANCY JACKETS

Moments before I went totally insane,
discovered writing would ease my pain.
Part of the journey from rags to riches,
Broken bones, sutures and stitches.
Rubber rooms, busted knuckles.
Fancy jackets—straps and buckles.
Hope my writings can be retribution.
For years I've wasted in these institutions.

3 HELD CAPTIVE

OBSTRUCTED VIEW

Been hard, just lifting my head.
Across the paper, I push the lead.
Hope a spiritual awakening happens soon.
Feel so alone in this crowded room.

Surroundings rough… language foul.
Hear my prayers? I wonder how.
Troubles around…try to stay clear.
Listen for your voice…can barely hear.

Engulfed. Noise pollution.
Finding prayer, only solution.
Close to empty, half a cup
Please lift my spirit up.

Barred windows. Two rows of fences.

This chapter, rattled my senses.

Struggling, need help from you

dealing with, this obstructed view.

ANOTHER LOST SOUL

Must admit, sin, fun for a season.
When it was over, homeless and freezing.
Never having the ability to cope.
Running from life. Strung out on dope.

Walking around just another lost soul.
Dark side of the city took its toll.
Concrete, asphalt, brick and stone.
The city streets became my home.

Marijuana, alcohol, heroin and crack.
Moment of Grace brought me back.
Spirit of the Universe watched over me.
In active addiction I was too blind to see.

Thank you for this cell. I rest my head.
Hadn't put me here—surely be dead.
Trust and faith, I must enhance.
Without it—Don't stand a chance.

THE NEXT PAGE

Sitting in the dark.
Trying to write.
Waiting for the muse.
To turn on the light.

Things that happen.
Do so for a reason.
Every bud blossoms.
In its due season.

Life in paradise
Today is a cage.
Waiting for the muse,
to prepare the next page.

YARD CALL

Inmates get let out of their pen.
Head to the yard, hook up with a friend.
Have one hour to relieve our stress.
Rest of the time our bunks we press.

On their life, old timers reflect back.
Hour each day as they walk the track.
Just a moment frowns turn to smiles.
Walking circles they travel for miles.

Short-timers lift weights till they fall.
Only one hour, then its yard call.
Time to head back into the cell.
Most can't handle it—a living hell.

LIVING INSIGHT

Newcomers are scared.
Prison has its effect.
Lifers kick back.
Demand their respect.
I cannot forget.
A lifer's cry at night.
One last chance.
Better do things right.

FREE AT HEART

Walls are cold.
Affecting how I feel.
I sit alone.
Behind this steel.
Captivity is here.
Freedom's out there
Seeking serenity
Window to nowhere.
Turquoise sky
Straddling my view.
Beautiful world,
I long for you.
Distant dreams
Mountains of doubt
Anticipate the day
they let me out.
Nothing like
A brand-new start
Until that day comes…
Free at heart.

PUPPET MASTER

Blistering Wind.
Snowy train ride.
Straight through the mountain.
Time on my side.

Pen has awakened.
Stealing a moment's fate.
Escaping captivity.
Not a minute too late.

Pride and ego
take one on the chin.
As the puppet master
stirs the pot again.

Stress and uncertainty
Peaks in the cloud.
Racing towards the core
Fears roaring so loud.

HELD CAPTIVE

Many miles from a place called home.
In the middle of a journey unknown.
Lost, losing concept of time.
Fallen into a dream of mine.

Leaving behind a world I endure.
Serenity provoked visions so pure
Mountain summits, cool running streams.
Held captive in my wildest dreams.

Giant rainbow piercing the clouds.
Arch angels gather in crowds.
Constructed beneath the realm of love.
Place this perfect comes from above.

Vibrant planet awakens before me.
Full of life roaming free.
Birds with broken wings learn to fly.
Place where children never cry.

Ailments healed with a gentle rain.

Subtle breeze removes our pain.

Peace and joy ruling the land.

Prayer guides the shepherd's hand.

A SENSE OF FREEDOM

To escape solitude that I felt.
Walls around me had to melt.
Using mind, body, and soul.
Allow my character to play its role.

Take lead in this screen play.
Beats time in the cell today.
Stage set. It's the open road.
Headed off to lighten my load.

Progress beyond these fences.
First thing noticed were my senses.
Suddenly vision became so clear.
Sounds of life echo in my ear.

Day is young. Freshness I smell.
Several miles from the gates of hell.
Perched myself on rumbling hills.
Two more senses needing thrills.

Natural stream—taste from there.

Autumn breeze brushes my hair.

Feel the richness of Mother Earth.

Today, freedom's been given birth.

VOYAGE

Travelling across a stormy sea.
Try to resist this force upon me.
Amazed how hard gravity pulls.
I've broken everyone's rules.

Climbing through life, reached plateau.
Crumbling walls, the valley below.
Once again plummeted from a stance.
Off on a journey. Search for a chance.

New beginning. Mended Heart
Stronger foundation. Brand new start.
Consumed by the world—its wicked ways.
Searching for kinder… gentler rays

Chasing a dream. Following the sun.
Over the horizon. Life on the run.
Vision distorted. Destination unclear
Lonely pilgrim. In search of a frontier.

4 CLUELESS

SAND AND SURF

Boss and I.
Had words today.
Gave him the finger.
Went on my way.

Escape from reality
within her swells.
Admiring children
gather their shells.

Dance in the ocean.
Crabs nibble my toes.
Waiting on a wave.
Sunblock on my nose.

Hooray, restless soul!
Escaped nine to five.
Sand and surf.
Reminds me I'm alive.

DATING AT THE BEACH

Down on the boardwalk, south of Main Street.
Another blind date. New lady to meet.
Met at a place called the Bearded Clam.
She imitated Rebecca; I played Sam.

Lying to her. She manipulated me.
Something exciting, premeditated ecstasy.
Weather was great. The beach, we roam.
Indulging conversation, headed for home.

Night still young; passion in the air.
Loved spanking her ass. She pulled my hair.
Hoping my soulmate arrives soon.
Reckless women, destroying my room.

THE SANDS OF DOOM

Wild nights.
Month of June.
Making love.
Sands of doom.

Lost emotions.
Just like a fiend.
She was married.
I was barely clean.

Making love.
Month of June.
Wild nights
Sands of doom.

She's in love.
Not with my brother.
It wasn't right.
Should have chosen another.

Wild nights.

Month of June.

Making love.

Sands of doom.

Fatal attraction.

The unforgiven.

Shock to the heart

Done the forbidden.

STRAIGHT DEMONIC

No surprise, my life's in disarray.
Listen to the thoughts, I had today.
For so long, perched upon this ledge.
Think it's time to jump over the edge.

Disregard precious goals and dreams.
Swim nude in the city's polluted streams.
Want to shoot coke, run naked through Baltimore.
Leave my sophisticated wife. Marry a whore.

Russian Roulette. Dance with a gun.
Bark at the moon. Murder the sun.
Origin of thoughts? Never can tell.
One thing's for sure: it'll be hot in hell.

HOPELESS ROMANTIC

Admire when I'm up
Compassion when I'm down
Appreciate my smile
Make love to my frown

Give total satisfaction
Truly do my part
Each and every one
Keys to my heart

Have a gentle spirit
That loves to flirt
When the relationship ends
Someone will get hurt

Seem to fall short
Of being the right guy
Have low self-esteem
I'm extremely shy

Too many disorders
More than I can count
Every woman I meet
Just have to mount

Extremely self-centered
Never get enough
A hopeless romantic
My sex, quite rough

Hard being monogamous
When so insecure
Want to be faithful
But addicted to more

PALE MOONS

Cashmere.

Black ties.

Countless trips.

Wine bottles.

Dinner dates.

Endless scripts.

Rental cars.

Hot tramps.

Loud tunes.

Sunrises.

Sunsets.

Pale moons.

PUNK PASSION

Drink and smoke,
Crash topless bars.
The boys and I,
Wrists have scars.

High top boots.
Long punky hair.
Love to fight.
Fuck everywhere.

Create a style.
Hell with fashion.
The boys and I,
We like thrashin'.

Girls are rockin'.
Party crashin'.
It's all because,
Punks have passion.

CAPTAIN JACK MORGAN

Objective sweet
Observed before
Captain Jack
Desired more
Lingering dame
Callous heart
Rocked world
Torn apart
Wrecked bed
Stolen truck
Abandoned note
Pleasant fuck
Fastened
Morning fog
Empty flask
Quivering dog

JANE DOE

Growing up, Jane, a tame child.
Coming of age, drove her wild.
Standing in heels, leather and lace.
Filling the void. Heart's an empty place.

Footprints embedded into the streets.
Fake smile for everyone she meets.
Pain hiding behind a pretty face.
Disease lying dormant, without a trace.

John Doe comes along abusing his power.
Searching for a soul, to rent by the hour.
Needing kicks, loving to be in control.
Purchased a disease that will take its toll.

Even though, he's home on time,
Ultimate price. Paid for his crime.
In devastation, he falls to his knees;
Learns he has a fatal disease.

CLUELESS

I have potential,
good intentions.
Everyone thinks I'm well.

Sometimes I lie,
cheat and steal.
Secrets to tell.

A cowboy
on this planet.
Bucking to be free.

Want a fix.
Gratification.
Desire's killing me.

World is clueless.
Will not find out.
Until I make a scene.

I have lost it.

Spun out of control.

Junkie, poet,

Sex fiend.

REHAB

First lost my spirit
Then sold my soul
After years of addiction
Finally lost control

Obsessive, compulsive
Resentment and fear
My own reflection
Shaped my tears

Had a few chances
Ran out of luck
Was once attractive
Now, ugly as fuck

Heart's growing callous
Mind's a darkening slab
Time for a new beginning
So I'm off to rehab

5 OBSESSED WITH A GHOST

LIMBO

New way of life

At times is ironic

One day I'm spiritual

Next day, demonic

Recovering addict

Few months clean

Writing heaven and hell

While stuck in between

BIGGER THAN ME

Could someone from the past
Be making a stand?
I am often surprised
What flows through my hand

My writings have become
What they are just because
What I don't comprehend
I think my pencil does

Maybe the spirits
Have a message for me
There's more to life
Than we're allowed to see

Open-mindedness
Reaching new heights
Making amends
Setting things right

SUBMISSIVE

There's a fragment all alone
I'm desperate to find its home
Needs rhythm and matching verse
Incomplete poem a deadly curse
Writing. I leave nothing on the table
Structured poetry keeps me stable
Quiet my mind. The madness ceases
Universe mends my scattered pieces

EDITOR'S LIST

Struggling with sobriety
Create a new addiction
Writing in a world
Both fact and fiction.

Editor gave me a list
Things I should fear
At the very top it read
"Book will ruin your career."

Told her it's about passion
Extremely hard to resist
No control over the world
Or a career that doesn't exist.

It's only through death
Poets can reach fame
I must work diligently
At what's going to remain.

I WONDER, TOO

What does love
mean to you?
Something we say
Or something we do

It feels so good
To say and hear
effect it has
May bring a tear

Word can make us happy
Or sad and blue
When you're not around
I think of you

What does this word
Mean to you?
Don't worry, Lovey
I wonder, too

HEART'S DESTINY

Longing for your smile
Sweetest one I've known
Listening for your voice
My defenses blown
Aching for your touch
Stirs my soul and heart
Sensing a closeness
Even when we're apart
Believing some things in life
Are simply meant to be
You are my soulmate
My heart's destiny

VIRGIN INNOCENCE

A blessing or a curse?
He desires to be her first
To penetrate her virgin skin
Where a man has never been

She's the universe. Captivating sight.
Goddess of poems. Portrait of light
Innocence. Barely come of age
Love she shares, a blinding rage

Intuition coincides with his plan
Wants this boy to become a man
The desert needs to quench its thirst
She longs for him to be her first

Anticipation. Could no longer endure
Bodies crash. Fall to the floor
Heat of passion sounds the alarms
Together. Found in each other's arms

WINTER'S STORM

Winter storm has run aground
No movement—not a soul found
Frigid weather, trees gracefully bow
Distant sounds from screeching owl.

Lying here, hidden from winter's sky
We are all alone, Lovey and I
Clothes scattered through the halls
Shadows perform across the walls.

Willing to give, we also receive
One surrenders. The other retrieves
Separating reality from within a dream
Evening's given way to a romantic scene.

Raging fire. Its sheltered light.
Together, madness surfs the night
Our morals, we refuse to face
Frost keeps flames, dancing in place.

Snow drifts, piling so deep
Passion provoking. Secrets to keep
Consumed by lust, covered with sin
Hope tomorrow, it snows once again.

OBSESSED WITH A GHOST

Cool ocean breeze
Planets align just right
Tide rushing in
Fading into night.

Cross your boundaries
Feel warm inside
Wet as the ocean
I lay you beside.

Making love to you
Such exotic places
Penetrating outer limits
Your most inner spaces.

Passion so hot
Leaves emotional scars
Multiple orgasms
Beneath a galaxy of stars.

Become so aroused
Souls begin to scream!
Awakening me from within
Wet and wild dreams.

Stuck in a frenzy
Searching around
Rush back to sleep
Nowhere to be found.

Obsessed with a ghost
Preparing for the day
Our paths cross tonight
I'll ask Lovey to stay.

6 HIGHER FREQUENCIES

ENIGMA

Searching for identity that's eluded me.

Needing validation. Long to be free.

Manic side breeds an artistic view.

Willingness to create, pulls me through.

Breaking shackles binding to the ground.

Inside my writings, identity must be found.

The vices I use, no longer hold.

Path I walk, continues to unfold.

Stuck in an enigma; eliminate the tears.

Knock down walls. Confront my fears.

To endure this journey, playing a role.

I will place identity upon my soul.

HUMILITY

Haze is thick
Fog settled in
Six years since
Entrusting my pen

Kind of ironic
Spiritually dead
Expedition
Unspoken words said

Effectively powerless
Unequipped for the day
Black and white
Bleeding shades of gray

Selfish shortcuts
Attempts to control
Compulsive desires
Consuming my soul

Addiction takes hold
Unwilling to feel
Twisted reality
Delusions seem real

Hyperactivity
Mind racing around
Bipolar disorder
Swinging up and down

Recovery's process
It's not a race
Save my ass
Not my face

Experienced stability
With all its glory
Doctor's medication
Parts of the story

Pride and ego

Submerged in sand

Through humility's

Outstretched hand

85

EXTREME CONDITIONS

Young writer tries to publish a book.
Talented musician created a hook.
Actor learns how to perform for you.
Painter tries to capture her view.

Hungry and poor, they live in their cars,
Battered and bruised with emotional scars.
One thing in common. An amazing feat,
Struggling—trying to make ends meet.

Not one born with a silver spoon—
Rise above rain and clouds of doom.
Journey is long. Souls have been torn.
Under extreme conditions, stars are born.

AT THE CROSSROADS

Promising artist. Goals and plans.
Several books. Handful of fans.
Conquer demons. Continue to give.
Lose all hope—the desire to live.

Call to the artist. Bleed his heart.
Critics said poetry's a dying art.
Can't drop the ball. Lay down and nap.
Time to place poetry back on the map.

Mostly cloudy, dark, gloomy day.
When the poet says all there is to say.
Taking wrong roads to bitter ends.
Sacrificing love of family and friends.

Reestablish himself. Learn how to cope.
Or drown in alcohol and return to dope.
Crawling, scratching, trying to break through.
A world anticipating someone fresh and new.

FILLED WITH PRIDE

Courage and Fear
Hate and Love
Given in—Risen above
Chaos and Peace
Happiness and Sorrow
Made money—Had to borrow
Drunk and Sober
Stolen and Gave
Been free—Also a slave
Lost and Found
Wrong and Right
Ran away—Stayed to fight
Sick and Well
Smiled and Cried
Been ashamed—Filled with pride

SURRENDER

These troubled times
Can barely cope
Calling on you
Inspiration and hope

This is the struggle
That's stirring within
Forgive me creator
I battle with sin

Flesh marches forward
Soul retreats back
Spiritual warfare
I am under attack

Today it's confirmation
My heart longs for
Seek deliverance from
Endless search for more

Fighting a battle
You've already won
In my surrender
Your will be done

WEAPON OF CHOICE

Retrieving messages within our souls
Dispensing contents, black as coals
Receive great joy, watching one flow
Hold them tight, never wanting to let go

Emptiness without presence in hand
Poets have used them to make a stand
They've brought abundance of wealth
For another's means of expressing himself

Writers, it becomes their voice
Their universal weapons of choice
Always close, never out of sight
The calling may occur deep in the night

Poets and their weapons must become one
Striving towards excellence, just for fun
Keeping them from becoming bored
The pen is mightier than the sword

ANSWERING THE CALL

Dream is real. The road, long.
Piercing a world in which I don't belong.
All the soul possesses, I'll have to give.
To obtain this goal; a reason to live.
Inspiration is life. This vast universe.
Life is short. No time to rehearse.
To be original, willing to go anywhere.
Above loneliness, reaching beyond despair.
Despite shortcomings, I try my best.
Bleeding heart's being put to the test.
Pen and pad become traveling gear.
Never in one spot more than a year.
Being submissive to one's fate.
Deep passion, this desire to create.
Feel a responsibility to do my part.
Penetrate the world of literary art.

OUR BOOK

A bond of trust. The Universe and I.
She has me writing. I wonder why.
Reflecting back, first heard the call.
Summer ending… with traces of fall.

Pulled me aside, revealing her power.
Remember being lost, consumed by the hour.
First poem we wrote, "Heaven on Earth."
A special day. Writer given birth.

Seems to be a task at hand.
Is it mine or something she planned?
Poetry—I am fish on a hook.
Will it be possible to publish our book?

For us to be found, truly great.
Getting published; it takes some fate.
Whether or not they live to see light.
Poetry gets me through the night.

PRESTIGE

So depressed. Filled with internal rage.

Stems from disappointment. The empty page.

Some think it's madness. I say, "No way."

Been here hours. Willing to spend the day.

Looking for reason to turn frown into smile.

Something inspirational that endures a while.

Don't know if it's destiny. A thing called fate.

Hope to write something misinterpreted as great.

Ultimate goal is to obtain a Pulitzer Prize.

Earn power and prestige. Help others rise.

MEDITATION

Sit peacefully. Silent love for my timidness.

Retreat from aggression found in bitterness.

It's self-induced. Altered state of mind.

Nothing exists. The world, truly blind.

Soul calm and collected under indigo sky.

Shortcomings and achievements pass me by.

Thoughts can be an ocean, the rolling waves.

Don't attach to them. They reach shallow graves.

A time and space, I don't celebrate or grieve.

Sit with my thoughts until they're ready to leave.

A SPIRITUAL SOLUTION

Fan base. Poetry books.
Deep meditation. Bubbling brooks.
Grassy pasture. Tiny finches.
Isolated trail. Lonely benches.

Rainy day. Simple words.
Wildflowers. Hummingbirds.
Health and prosperity. Family. Friends.
Internal Journey. Hope never ends.

Found respect. Absence of drama.
Praised Jesus. Worshiped Dalai Lama.
Sounds crazy. Maybe misunderstood.
True enlightenment. It's all good.

I don't have to be right or wrong.
Just for today—emotionally strong.
Not about religion. Mere contribution.
Finally developed a spiritual solution.

NATURE'S POWERS

Summer's heat. Busy wings.

Mosquito bites. Bee stings.

Rip curls. Undertows.

Shifting tides. Current flows.

Autumn's glory. The walnut.

Buck meets doe. Season's rut.

Snow bunnies. Winter thrills.

Mountaintops. Rolling hills.

April rains. May flowers.

Spring blooms. Nature's powers.

HIGHER FREQUENCIES

Creative space
Amazing weather
Elusive fragments
Mending together

Vibrant marsh
Sheltering wildest fowl
Parked on a bridge
Straddling Lewes Canal

Horizon straight
With a gentle curve
The powers that be
I'm here to observe

Silence quiets the soul
Cleansing my inner layer
Acknowledgement of creation
Has become a simple prayer

Through stillness and solitude
Faith allows me to believe
There's a higher frequency
I tune in and receive

99

7 SILENCE IS DEATH

WHEN COLORING A POEM

Remain openminded
To the art, be true
If it's meant to be
The muse will find you

Because life and art
Make a wonderful mixture
Artists coloring poems
For fans that read pictures

So, tell your story
Allow the reader to see
You've followed your heart
With words, created imagery

Visual art can speak
Make your message clear
When you paint a picture
Make it one they can hear

NAKED

Press through the fear
Make the poetry good
Reveal a bit more
Than you think you should

Don't scratch the surface
Make sure to dig deep
You're not the only one
Who sold their soul cheap

Just be true to the art
There's no need to fake it
When you follow the muse
You will end up naked

LOVE

Love's elusive, hard to find.
A raw emotion that makes us blind.
A tiny ember, turned raging fire.
Love is what our hearts desire.

Once its arrow pierces your heart.
Willingness comes to do your part.
Finding your way through a maze.
Love is eternal, more than a phase.

Attraction to a person or thing.
Totally consumed by the joy they bring.
While penetrating all my defenses.
It was love that conquered all senses.

SILHOUETTE

Centered in a midnight sky
Deepest, darkest blue—
The moonlight is casting
A silhouette of you

Our time together
The love we share
Something so precious
Reached beyond compare

Extremely blessed
Experiencing something so true
I've waited my entire life
For these moments with you

DESTINY

Our deepest pain
Learned to divide
Revealing a past
Could no longer hide
I was here for you
You were there for me
Breaking shackles
Together, we are free
Transforming frowns
Into beautiful smiles
We were willing to go
Those extra miles
Together we walk
Hand in hand
Love so pure
Had to be planned

MOST PROMISING NIGHT

Upholding an image
Of beauty and grace
I was slowly recovering
From a dark, empty space

Rose from the ashes
Lost—burnt out life
She's all I dreamed of
Candidate for a wife

Her spirit uplifting
Mine, kind of down
Together, we laugh
Apart, we frown

A stable woman
Taste and fashion
Me? Extreme manic
Love with passion

Her true phoenix
My lonesome dove
Peace in our heart
Compares to our love

Reached ultimate goal
Most promising night
Made love on the bridge
Then took our last flight

Found a soul mate
My life got better
We left this poem
Then died together

A poetic justice
Ending like this
Over the edge
Engaged in a kiss

SILENCE IS DEATH

Awaiting a spark
To ignite eternal flame
Something with passion
Depth to my name

Silence is death
Back's against the wall
Poet's last stand
Not silent at all

Final hour has come
I've been pronounced dead
So, think eternal life
As my spoken words read

Family and friends
Nothing as true
Love and acceptance
Received from you

Life to the fullest

No worry or regrets

Hope in sunrises

Peace as sun sets

Hold your head high

No reason to mourn

As I lay here at rest

My poetry lives on

SOUTH OF SERENITY

My right hand builds
While the other destroys
My desperate soul hates
What the hot flesh enjoys
Living in a hardened world
With this fragile mind
It's South of Serenity
That was easy to find

The end.

MY DAILY PRAYER

The Powers that Be,

Take my will and my life.
Guide me in my journey.
Show me how to live.

I offer all of myself,
Good and bad.
I pray that you will remove
Every defect of character
That stands in the way
Of my usefulness
To you and my fellows.

Grant me strength
As I go out
And do your bidding.

I pray only for the knowledge
Of your will
And the power to carry it out.

(Thanks Bill W.)

ABOUT THE AUTHOR

Ray Hamilton, born and raised in Baltimore, Maryland, (Remington/Hampden area) now resides in Lewes, Delaware. His passions include spending time in the beauty of nature's creations, writing poetry, and house painting.

Ray began his journey as a poet through his inability to deal with the ups and downs (mostly downs) of life. Incarcerated in a prison of mental illness and trauma led him first to fear, then to addiction, and finally to freedom through spiritual growth and therapeutic writing.

Inspired by the writings of Dr. Suess, Ray found the Universe's healing through pain, inventory, and expression.